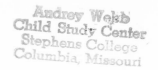

Let's Look at More Tracks

About the Book

The identification of animals through their tracks is a fascinating study. In this book, as in Ann Kirn's companion book *Let's Look at Tracks*, preschool and primary-grade children are encouraged to sharpen their observation skills. An animal's trail is shown, along with a textual description of the tracks to point out specific details. The young reader uses these clues to determine the animal that made the trail. Then, by turning the page, he sees a picture of the animal and reads about the animal. Included are a rabbit, skunk, deer, beaver, opossum, bear, otter, porcupine, raccoon, and fox.

LET'S LOOK AT MORE
TRACKS

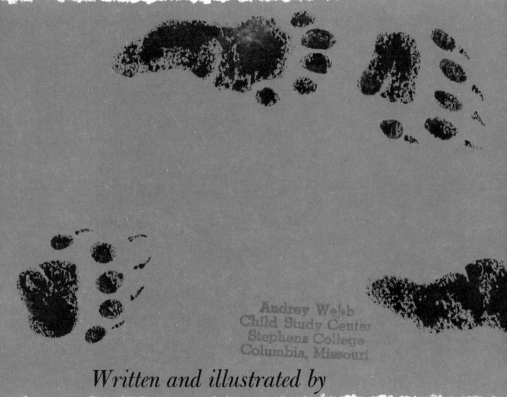

Written and illustrated by
ANN KIRN

G. P. PUTNAM'S SONS   NEW YORK

For Amy and Jay

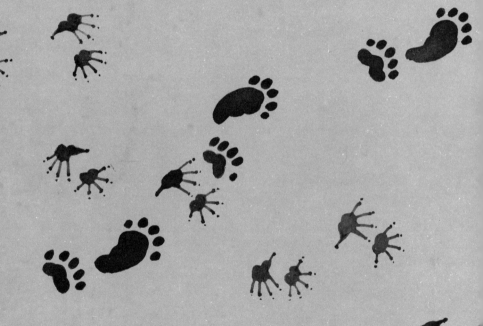

Copyright © 1970 by Ann Kirn

Let's Look at More Tracks

Tracks are footprints
pressed into soft earth
or sand or snow.

Some are flat-footed prints.

Others are toe prints,
and others are toenail prints.

You can find tracks in a park,
in a garden, in a woods,
on a beach, or beside a road.

In fact, you can find tracks
almost anywhere that animals go.

Tracks give you clues
about the animals
that made the tracks.

This book has pictures of tracks.

The pictures will help you guess
what animals made the tracks.

After a snowy night,
you may see these tracks.

An animal was hopping about,
looking for apples
under the snow.

Its long ears were cocked,
and its nose twitched.

It was trying to hear
and smell a dog
or other animal out hunting.

Look at the trail.

The tracks are in groups of four.

Big hind feet went first,
making deep prints
in the soft snow.

Then two little front paws
came down behind them.

These tracks belong to . . .

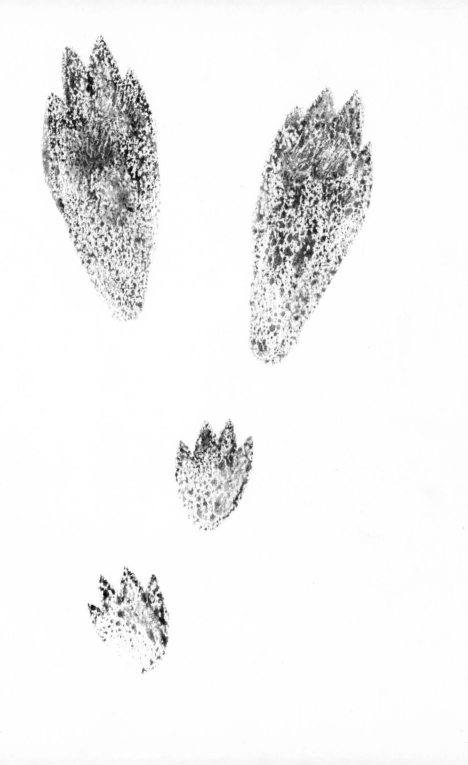

. . . a rabbit.

She is called a cottontail.

The underside of her tail
is as soft and as white
as a ball of cotton.

In the spring,
mother rabbit pulls out
her soft fur to make a nest.

She pulls grass and leaves
over the nest
to hide her bunnies.

Watch mother rabbit
as she nibbles lettuce
in a spring garden.

If she sees you, she will stop.

Don't go too close.

Then you won't see anything
but her bobbing white tail.

9

When you walk along
by the side of a road,
look for flat-footed prints.

This animal is not very big.

Still, it is not afraid
of other animals.

Others may be afraid of it.

It takes care of itself
by spraying a bad smell.

Look at the prints
of its hind feet.

They are bigger and flatter
than the prints
of its front feet.

Each track shows five toes,
but the claws are not seen
in the hind footprints.

These tracks belong to ...

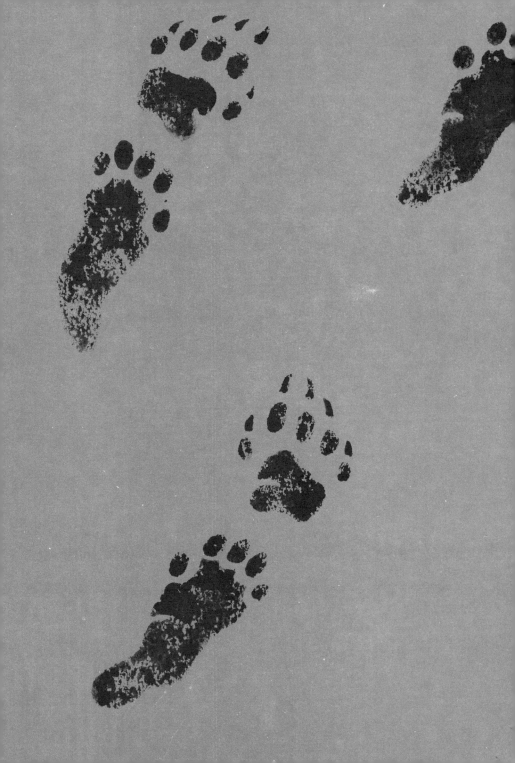

. . . a skunk.

See her walking
in the spring grass.

She stops to smell a violet,
then walks on
to an old tree stump.

She is hunting for insects
and their eggs.

A skunk will also eat mice,
frogs, and little snakes.

Her long black fur
has two white stripes.

These stripes run
from her head
to the tip of her tail.

Do not frighten a skunk.

If her bushy tail goes up,
you'd better run away fast.

13

You may find these tracks
beside some bigger ones
just like them.

The toenail prints were made
by a baby as it ran along
beside its mother.

When three weeks old,
it hid under the bushes
while its mother was away.

Now it goes browsing with her.

They nibble twigs and buds
and plants growing in a pond.

The baby animal walks
on the tips of its toes.

Look at the trail.

See how its hind feet step
on the tracks of its front feet.

These tracks belong to . . .

... a deer.

This young fawn
is a white-tailed deer.

The underside of his tail
is white like his mother's.

His spotted coat
makes it hard for you
to see him.

If he sees you,
he will stand still.

Then away he will leap
through the tall trees.

When he is four months old,
he will lose his spots.

Fawns like to jump and leap,
playing tag with one another.

They also like to swim
and splash in the water.

17

If you see tree stumps
beside a stream,
look for tracks.

You may find some tracks
going down into the water.

A smart animal used trees
to build a dam
and make a pond.

Then it built its house
in the pond.

This animal swims well.

See the prints of the webs
of its hind feet.

These webs help it swim.

On land it is clumsy,
for its legs are short
and it drags a wide tail.

These tracks belong to ...

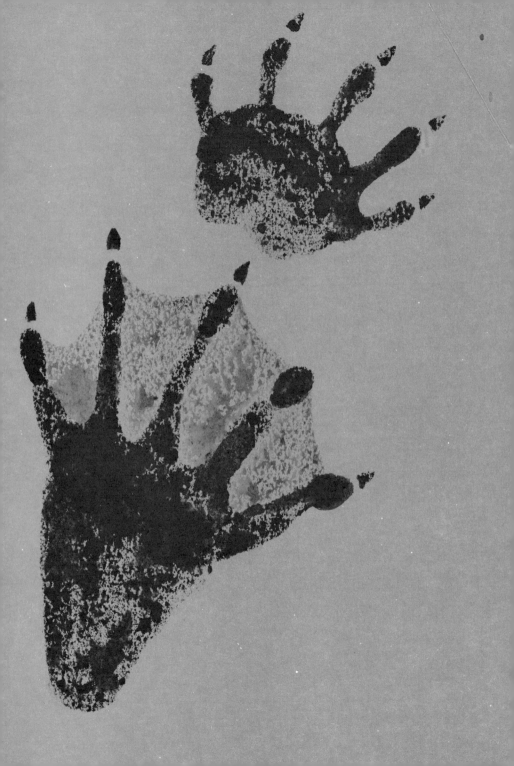

. . . a beaver.

The beaver combs his fur coat
with his hind feet.

He makes the coat shed water
by rubbing it with oil
from glands under his tail.

He uses his tail
as a rudder for swimming
and as a brace for standing.

He uses his tail as a signal.

He can signal other beavers
by slapping it in the water.

Mother beaver keeps her kits
in a nest of twigs and bark.

Someday they will build
their own dams and houses.

Then they, too, will be
as **busy as beavers.**

Early on a dewy morning,
you may find these footprints
in the damp earth.

This long, fat animal hunts
during the night.

It looks for insects, frogs,
chickens, eggs, and fruits.

Its legs are very short,
so it waddles when it walks.

See the flat-footed prints
of the animal's hind feet.

A big toe sticks out
like your thumb.

This big toe helps the animal
to climb up trees and vines.

Look at the print made
by a dragging tail.

These tracks belong to . . .

22

...an opossum.

An opossum is a little bigger
than a cat.

His white face is pointy
with a piglike snout.

His tail is bare and scaly
like the tail of a rat.

See him hang by his tail.

He also uses his tail
to carry leaves and twigs.

Babies are carried
in their mother's pouch
until five weeks old.

Then they ride on her back,
wrapping their tails
around her tail.

When an opossum is afraid,
it makes believe it is dead.

25

Look for these tracks
in a state or national park.

They were made by an animal
that just climbed down a tree
and waddled after its mother.

Its flat-footed tracks are big,
but they are not as big
as its mother's tracks.

If its mother is busy,
she will send this baby
back up the tree.

The front paws have small palms.

The palms of the hind feet
are long and flat.

All of the toes have claws.

They are short claws and often
do not show up in the prints.

These tracks belong to ...

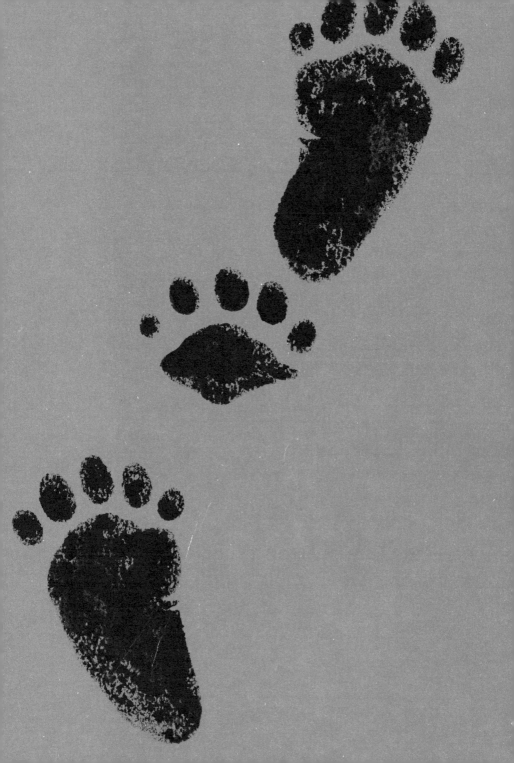

...a bear cub.

His furry coat is black,
but he may have a brother
with a furry brown coat.

Bears like to romp and play
during the warm summertime.

On cold winter days, however,
they would rather sleep.

Black bears like to eat,
and they will eat insects,
berries, grass, and fish.

They love to rob a beehive
of its honey.

They will even eat the bees.

See this cub sitting up,
begging someone to feed him.

But the park ranger says,
"Do not feed the bears."

Along the snowy banks
of a frozen stream,
you may find these tracks.

You also may see a snowy path,
hard and slippery.

A playful animal climbed up
just to enjoy sliding down.

This animal loves to slide
as much as it loves to swim.

Webs between its toes
help it to swim very fast.

The webs cannot be seen
in the snowy footprints.

But you can see all five toes
with their sharp claws.

You can also see
the tail-drag on the side.

These tracks belong to ...

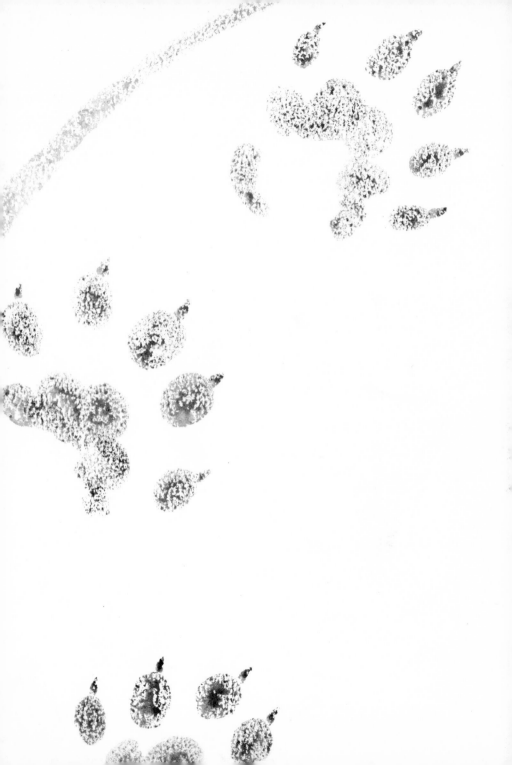

...an otter.

See the playful otter
sliding in the snow.

His long, slim body helps him
to slide and swim.

He can outswim any fish
and often catches small fish.

In early spring, mother otter
has as many as five pups.

She keeps them in a den
for about three months.

Then she brings them out
to play and swim and hunt.

On sunny days, mother otter
uses her sharp claws
to comb the pups' fur.

Then they take their turns
and comb her furry coat.

If you see these tracks
under a tall pine tree,
look up into the tree.

You may see an animal
with sharp-pointed quills.

No one likes to get close
to this animal.

If it slaps you with its tail,
you will be stuck
by those long quills.

Look at the trail.

See how the toes turn in
and how the hind feet step
in the front footprints.

Each front foot has four toes,
and each hind foot has five.

All the toes have long claws.

These tracks belong to . . .

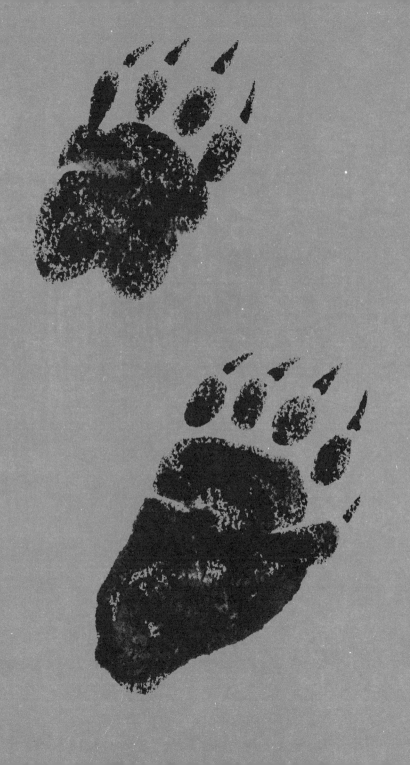

... a porcupine.

A porcupine has a big body
and short legs.

This makes him look clumsy
as he waddles along.

The porcupine is too lazy
to make a nest or leafy bed
to use as a home.

He makes his home
in an evergreen tree.

He eats the bark of the tree
as he climbs up to his home.

The mother porcupine
has one fat baby.

Even when he is very little,
the baby can climb
and can slap his quilly tail.

So watch out for Baby Porky.

37

You can find these tracks
in a desert, on a beach,
or by a woodland stream.

This animal lives
in many kinds of places.

On cold winter days,
it curls up for a nap.

It covers its black nose
with a bushy tail
ringed with black and white.

This animal has long toes.

The toes are used as fingers
to pick fruits and shellfish.

Look at the tracks.

See how the print
of a front paw looks
almost like a hand print.

These tracks belong to ...

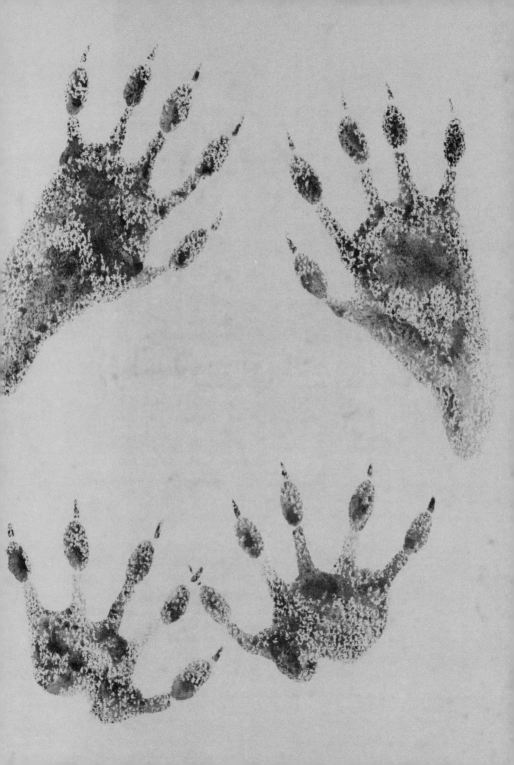

...a raccoon.

See him at the water's edge.

He is washing his food
before he eats it.

He will eat almost anything.

He likes nuts, fruits,
and corn, but most of all
he likes eggs and honey.

He looks as if he is wearing
a black mask on his face.

He even looks like a robber
as he robs a nest of its eggs
or a beehive of its honey.

Mother raccoon lifts her kits
by the backs of their necks.

Soon the babies are walking
behind her as she noses along,
hunting supper for her kits.

41

These are the tracks
of an animal
that runs on its toes.

It is not easy
to follow the tracks.

This animal is a sly one.

It will run back
over its footprints.

It will make a sharp turn
or run along a fence top
or dash through a stream.

Look at the tracks.

See the clear prints
of the toes.

The hind feet are set down
where the front feet went,
making one line of prints.

These tracks belong to ...

...a fox.

The smart red fox stops.

He stands still for a minute.

Then he is off and away
before you can get a good look.

He is a handsome animal
with his sleek reddish coat
and bushy white-tipped tail.

He eats fruits, berries,
insects, rabbits, and mice.

Mother fox keeps her pups
in a den among the rocks.

Father fox helps her
to teach the pups
about hunting for food.

He also teaches them
how to trick anyone
who might try to follow them.

Look on a beach
close to the tide line.

You may find these prints
in the damp sand
of a sand castle.

You may also see a trail
of prints going on
down to the water.

This animal usually walks
on its hind paws.

Today it was playfully
walking on its front ones.

Look at each print.

See the four fingerprints
and the fat thumbprint.

The thumb helps the animal
to pick up things.

These tracks belong to ...

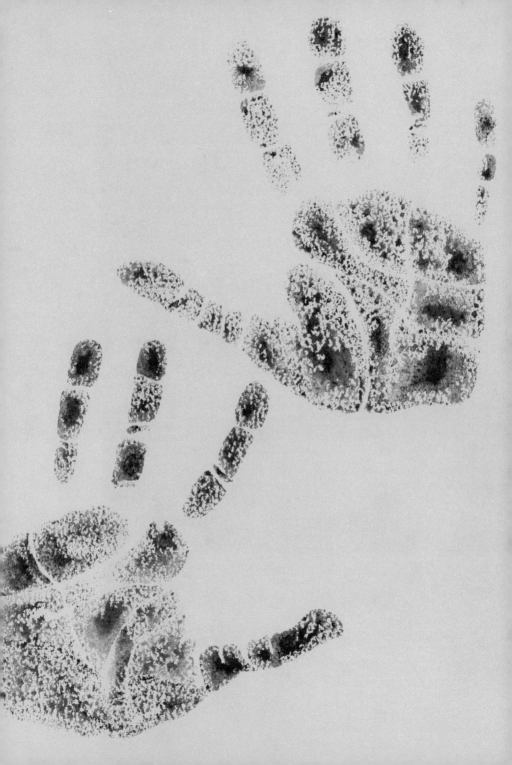

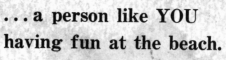 **...a person like YOU having fun at the beach.**

The Author-Artist

ANN KIRN was born in Missouri and studied art in Chicago, St. Louis, and Los Angeles. She has received a Master of Arts degree from Columbia University and for many years has taught in the fine arts department of Florida State University. She makes her home in Tallahassee, Florida. Miss Kirn has written and illustrated many children's books.

DATE DUE

MAY 0 3 2012	